Who Is It?

This book belongs to

_____

Who Is It?
A Language Learning Book for Wonderful Kids with Autism

PEC Books. ™
Twin Taurus Publishing ™

PECBooks.com
TwinTaurusPublishing.com

ISBN-10: 1614240019
ISBN-13: 978-1-61424-001-3

Library of Congress Control Number: 2011943151

Who Is It?

The ability to ask questions is a fundamental life skill. Asking questions not only enhances a child's learning potential, but is also critical to his or her safety and independence. Imagine living a single day without the capacity to identify new people in the world around you. "Who is it?" is a question critical to the social comfort and safety of every child.

This uniquely effective picture book is the cooperative effort of Parents, Experts, and Children (PEC). It is designed to teach wonderful kids with developmental disorders like Autism Spectrum Disorders by minimizing learning interference elements and making use of the extraordinary gifts so many challenged children possess. Repeated readings help demonstrate the purpose of asking questions and encourage children to ask independently.

Books by
Parents, Experts, and Children

PEC Books are learning tools created by Parents, Experts, and Children. PEC projects reflect the experience, research, and wisdom of those most familiar with the challenges and opportunities that come with early childhood education and special needs. PEC Books are specifically designed for use with children facing developmental disabilities, but are beneficial to children of all abilities. Parents and educators can increase the effectiveness of this book by clearly demonstrating the use of questions in casual, real-life situations.

Who is it?

It's a policeman.

Who is it?

It's an astronaut.

Who is it?

It's a garbage man.

Who is it?

It's a librarian.

Who is it?

It's a plumber.

Who is it?

It's an artist.

Who is it?

It's a gardener.

Who is it?

It's a florist.

Who is it?

It's a construction worker.

Who is it?

It's a coach.

Who is it?

It's a chef.

Who is it?

It's a bus driver.

Who is it?

It's a janitor.

Who is it?

It's a teacher.

Who is it?

It's a mailman.

Who is it?

It's a fire fighter.

A note of thanks...

To the parents, experts, and children who have contributed to this project both directly and indirectly, a tremendous debt of gratitude is owed. These books would not be possible without your interest, ideas, time, and effort.

To the heroic women and men who devote their lives and careers to the advancement of children with developmental challenges, no words could ever convey our appreciation. Your dedication and constant efforts make a very real difference in the fight to save children whose gifts might otherwise be overlooked and whose potential would likely be discarded. Thank you.

12098753R00020

Made in the USA
Charleston, SC
11 April 2012

Available online and in finer retail book outlets.

What Is It?

Books b
Parents, Experts, and Children

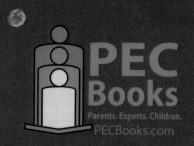

PEC Books
Parents. Experts. Children.
PECBooks.com

Look for other great titles for children with developmental challenges.

Twin Taurus
Publishing
TwinTaurusPublishing.com

ISBN-13: 978-1-61424-001-3 $12.50 USA

9 781614 240013

51250 >

Talking Planets
COMIC BOOK

The Night Problem

Written By **Jada Scott**